Disclaimer

Steven Krohn, © 2017 – All Rights Reserved

No part of this e-book may be reproduced, stored, or transmitted in any form or by any means including mechanical or electronic without prior written permission from the author.

While the author has made every effort to ensure that the ideas, statistics, and information presented in this eBook are accurate to the best of his/her abilities, any implications direct, derived, or perceived, should only be used at the reader's discretion. The author cannot be held responsible for any personal or commercial damage arising from communication, application, or misinterpretation of information presented herein.

All Rights Reserved.

Introduction – The Changing Dynamics of the Financial World

"At its core, Bitcoin is a smart currency, designed by very forward-thinking engineers. It eliminates the need for banks, gets rid of credit card fees, currency exchange fees, money transfer fees, and reduces the need for lawyers in transitions... all good things."

Peter Diamandis – Founder & Chairman of the X Prize Foundation

Well, that quote says it all there is to say about cryptocurrency – a digital currency that has taken the world by storm!

Only a few people might know this, but cryptocurrencies actually emerged as a by-product of another invention. *Satoshi Nakamoto,* the inventor of Bitcoin, the first ever and still the most important cryptocurrency in the world, never had any intention of inventing any form of currency. In 2008, Satoshi stated that he had developed a peer-to-peer electronic cash system. It was a digital cash system without any regulatory authority. This idea further led to the creation of cryptocurrency.

Who knew cryptocurrency would become a global phenomenon, a sensation that would shake the financial world down to its very core in just a few years!

Some might even say cryptocurrency is the biggest invention since the internet came into existence and changed the course of this world.

Even if you don't know what cryptocurrency is and how it works, you'd still know that its popularity is increasing like nothing else in this world. You must've asked yourself the question *why has this digital currency suddenly taken over the world*. It's an innocent question that has a lengthy answer – and that's what this book is for!

Yes, it is true cryptocurrency has altered the dynamics of this world radically. It has changed how international transactions used to take place, and it has changed the way businesses used to be conducted. As a matter of fact, it's continuing to do that and more for all the right reasons!

As complex as it is to transact by using cryptocurrency, it's always good to know that once you get a grip over its concepts, you can benefit from the most revolutionary invention of the recent times that has already penetrated the minds of the mainstream and is gradually becoming an integral part of the contemporary world.

So, what basically does cryptocurrency have to offer?

We know there's no risk of identity theft that exists in credit card transactions because cryptocurrency transactions are absolutely anonymous. We know there's the benefit of immediate settlement of a transaction without any involvement of third parties, making it super-easy and fast to complete the transfer of assets. Above all, there are no transaction fees involved in cryptocurrency trading, unless you engage a third party service to maintain your cryptocurrency wallet.

Here's a small astonishing fact for you to think about:

There are approximately 2.2 billion people in the world who have access to the internet or mobile phones, but they don't have any access to the traditional exchange systems. You might be surprised, but such people have already penetrated the cryptocurrency market. Kenya's M-PESA system is a mobile phone based service for money transfer. In 2017, M-PESA launched the facility of Bitcoin transfer, and now every 1 out of 3 Kenyans has a Bitcoin wallet!

People who invested in cryptocurrency in the early years of its inception now claim to have become millionaires. 50 Cent recently tweeted that his Bitcoins – which he had almost forgotten about – are now worth $8 million!

This is just the beginning. Cryptocurrency is destined to go higher than ever.

"In the long-term, Bitcoin moves above $500,000 within three years. Bets?"
John McAfee – Founder of the software and anti-virus company McAfee Associates

In this book, I'll start from the very beginning. In order to prove the importance and worth of cryptocurrency to the beginners, I'll introduce the currency and explain its purpose before moving on to the process of trading cryptocurrency. Further on, you'll be able to understand the mining process of Bitcoins and how you can maintain your crypto wallets. One of the major highlights of this book will be how and why digital marketing goes hand in hand with cryptocurrency, and how does it increase the value of cryptocurrency. *I hope you enjoy the read!*

Table of Contents

Chapter 1 – Cryptocurrency for Beginners 9

    1.1 – What Is Cryptocurrency? 9

    1.2 – Explaining Cryptocurrency 10

    1.3 – What Purpose Does Cryptocurrency Serve? 12

    1.4 – Defining the Value of Cryptocurrency 13

    1.5 – How Does Cryptocurrency Lure Investors 14

Chapter 2 – Trading Cryptocurrency 17

    2.1 – The First Lesson to Learn Before Trading 18

    2.2 – How to Choose a Cryptocurrency Exchange 19

Chapter 3 – The Cryptocurrency Market 23

    3.1 – The Growing Crypto Market Is a New Frontier of the Financial World 24

    3.2 – The Mighty Bitcoin 25

    3.3 – Understanding the Volatility of the Cryptocurrency Market .. 25

    3.4 – The Fear of Investing and the Risk Involved in the Crypto Market 26

    3.5 – What Is a Cryptocurrency Market Correction? 27

    3.6 – How Is a Cryptocurrency Market Correction Healthy 28

Chapter 4 – Initial Coin Offering (ICOs) 30

    4.1 – Getting Acquainted with the Concept of an ICO 30

    4.2 – How Does an ICO Work 31

    4.3 – Why Does ICOs Deserve Your Attention? 32

    4.4 – Attracting Potential Investors for an ICO 34

    4.5 – Why You Might Regret Not Investing in an ICO? 35

    4.6 – The Advantages of an ICO 35

Chapter 5 – Introducing Altcoin 37

- 5.1 – Why Do Altcoin Exist? 37
- 5.2 – Which Altcoin Is the Best Altcoin? 39
- 5.3 – Why Do People Keep Creating Altcoins? 40
- 5.4 – Some of the Most Popular Altcoins 41
  - 5.4.1 – Ethereum 42
  - 5.4.2 – Ripple 42
  - 5.4.3 – Litecoin 43
  - 5.4.4 – DASH 43
  - 5.4.5 – NEM 44
  - 5.4.6 – Ethereum Classic 44
  - 5.4.7 – Monero 45
  - 5.4.8 – Zcash 45
  - 5.4.9 – Decred 45
  - 5.4.10 – PIVX 46

Chapter 6 – Mining Coins 48
- 6.1 – Cryptocurrency Transactions 48
- 6.2 – The Art of Mining Coins 50
- 6.3 – Difficulty in Mining Coins 51

Chapter 7 – All You Need to Know About Staking Coins 54
- 7.1 – What Is Meant by Proof of Staking Coins? 55
- 7.2 – How Does the Process of Staking Coins Work? 55
- 7.3 – The Benefits of Staking Coins 56
- 7.4 – The Risks Involved in Staking Coins 57
- 7.5 – Popular Cryptocurrencies for Staking Coins 57
  - 7.5.1 – DASH 58
  - 7.5.2 – NEO 58

7.5.3 – OkCash 59

7.5.4 – PIVX 59

7.5.5 – NAV Coin 59

7.5.6 – Stratis 59

7.5.7 – Reddcoin 60

Chapter 8 – The Crypto Wallets 61

8.1 – Types of Cryptocurrency Wallets 63

8.1.1 – Hardware Wallets 64

8.1.2 – Software Wallets 65

8.1.3 – Paper Wallets 66

8.2 – Maintaining Crypto Wallets 66

8.3 – How to Choose the Best Crypto Wallet 67

Chapter 9 – Cryptocurrency & Marketing 69

9.1 – How Does Marketing Increase the Cryptocurrency Value 71

9.1.1 – Increases Visibility 71

9.1.2 – Establishes Authority 71

9.1.3 – Builds Rapport & Trustworthiness 72

9.2 – Digital Marketing for ICOs 73

9.2.1 – Optimize Your Website for Search Engines 74

9.2.2 – Put a Lot of Effort into Your White Paper 75

9.2.3 – Make a Credible Explainer Video 75

9.2.4 – Start E-Mail Marketing 75

9.2.5 – Use Social Media to Your Advantage 75

9.3 – Webinar – An Effective ICO Marketing Strategy 76

9.4 – Why Are Webinars an Effective Marketing Strategy for Launching an ICO 77

9.5 – The Importance of a Webinar 78

9.6 – Learn from Other Successful ICOs 79
9.7 – Digital Tokens 80
9.8 – Using Reddit as an ICO Marketing Tool 80
9.9 – How to Promote an ICO on Reddit 81
9.10 – Creating a Subreddit for Your Coin 82
9.11 – Engaging with Your Reddit Audience 83
    9.11.1 – Encourage Your Subreddit Followers and Attend Them 84
    9.11.2 – Dealing with Supporters' Feedback 84
    9.11.3 – Dealing with the Criticism 84
9.12 – Buying Up-Votes and Advertising on Reddit 85
Conclusion 86

Chapter 1 – Cryptocurrency for Beginners

It depends on how much you keep abreast with what's creating ripples in the world of modern business, but if you've tuned to business news media lately then you must've heard the name, "Cryptocurrency". The whole world pretty much keeps on talking about it!

If you aren't familiar with the term, then you certainly must've heard about "Bitcoin". Bitcoin is a type of cryptocurrency. Now, the thing is you can't really see any type of cryptocurrency. It might sound a little weird, but despite being used like conventional money that we're in habit of using, cryptocurrency does not exist in any *tangible form!*

1.1 – What Is Cryptocurrency?

Cryptocurrency is a digital currency. It's a decentralized currency. And it's mainly based on cryptography. The most popularly used and globally renowned cryptocurrency is Bitcoin. Almost everyone knows that Bitcoin was the first decentralized form of currency that came into existence.

When Bitcoin went online back in 2009, nobody really knew that cryptocurrency would become all the rage in the next few years. Now, it's called the *digital gold* in the industry.

Here's an interesting – and slightly frightening – piece of information. Satoshi Nakamoto, the inventor of Bitcoin, is more like a pen-name. *To this day nobody has ever come to know the mysterious man behind this name!*

It's true, since its inception, Bitcoin began to garner a lot of attention and the currency grew stronger every day because it had those remarkable features that could solve a number of inherent problems that were present in the traditional monetary system.

With no central authority to regulate it, these encrypted digital currencies, like Bitcoin, soon began to change hands electronically. Strange as it may seem, a cryptocurrency is a digital asset that will always exist and remain as data – regardless of who owns it and how much of it you have. This allows a person using cryptocurrency to send money like sending an email. This significantly reduces the time required for transferring funds from one place to another via banks. There are no middle-men involved and no credit cards. Your transactions are anonymous and bear no transaction fee unless you involve a third party to manage your account.

1.2 – Explaining Cryptocurrency

The use of cryptocurrency involves a master ledger for bookkeeping purposes called "Blockchain". A blockchain is public and is shared by a network of people who own the same type of coin, like Bitcoin. Thus, everybody, who owns a Bitcoin, has a copy of the ledger that stores all the transactions.

A transaction is not finalized until it has been added to the blockchain. Once recorded, the transaction becomes irreversible. During the time of a transaction, the units of the currency cannot be used by either side. This prevents fraud, duplication, and double spending. Since a blockchain has all the information about the mining activity, trades, and purchases of all the people who own the same cryptocurrency, it forms a community of trust.

Blockchain technology, which is the basis of cryptocurrency, offers a secure method to transfer funds and to identify each transaction. This is possible because each type of cryptocurrency is programmed using a very complex digital code.

Like conventional money, prices of digital currencies rise and fall depending on various factors and external forces. The media, news events, bad press, and government regulations contribute massively to price fluctuation that you notice in crypto trading. It's not just Bitcoin whose value constantly keeps on appreciating and depreciating. There are hundreds of altcoins that exist in the market today and all of them are affected by the same forces. The most widely traded variety of altcoins includes Litecoin, Ethereum, and Bitcoin Cash.

Someone who's new to this intriguing world of cryptocurrency might ask: where do we keep our digital currency.

Well, each user has an e-wallet that stores specific information. This information confirms the user as the owner of a particular cryptocurrency and allows you to transact with your coins.

1.3 – What Purpose Does Cryptocurrency Serve?

If truth be told, cryptocurrency was introduced to solve two major problems. The first problem was security threats and the second one was the protection of privacy.

Let's explore how the advent of cryptocurrency solved the first problem of security threats.

Using a decentralized currency allows users to keep a regular check on the public ledger (blockchain). This is an exceptionally secure system when compared to the traditional centralized monetary system. *You'll ask why.*

It is super-safe because if someone wants to hack a cryptocurrency, that genius would have to hack every single node at exactly the same time. Now that's just impossible because every type of cryptocurrency has millions of nodes! On the other hand, the traditional monetary system has only one node – the central bank. This makes it very easy for the professional hackers to hack, infiltrate, or manipulate the traditional monetary system. In fact, one of the reasons why the use of cryptocurrency has become so popular is that it's considered a *currency created for users and tracked by users!*

The anonymity of transactions solves the second problem cryptocurrency was intended to work out. Although the anonymity of crypto transactions is linked to illegal activities, it isn't certainly its purpose. Its purpose is just to protect your privacy.

The creators of Bitcoin were of the opinion that the government has no right to keep a check on your money – how much money you have and how do you spend it. These creators believed in a free financial market and advocated the idea that the government has absolutely no right to regulate these markets. That was the true ideology behind cryptocurrency.

1.4 – Defining the Value of Cryptocurrency
Does cryptocurrency have any value?

In short, YES!

Before I explain you the value of cryptocurrency, the one thing that you need to remember is that *value* of anything is always determined by the principles of demand and supply.

Let's take a look at an example to understand the value of cryptocurrency.

Imagine for a while that you own a luxurious property. When you try to determine its total cost you add up the money you spent on the land, the house itself, and all the furnishings. When you add up all these costs, you get the total cost of your property, i.e. $10 million.

Now, let's assume that there's an economic crisis and as result of it, the demand for your property in real estate market declines, *severely*. Your property was initially valued at $10 million, but since its value has declined, do you think you'd be able to sell it at a half price? The most obvious answer would be a solid NO, but what else can you do? There's no one interested in your property due to the prevailing crisis, so the best option you have is to sell it for $5 million.

Once the deal has been closed at $5 million, this amount becomes the current value of your property. The property that was once valued at $10 million is now only worth $5 million because the market always dictates the prices.

That was the end of the example. Now, how is that even remotely related to the value of cryptocurrency?

The people who have always criticized cryptocurrency say that the currency will fail eventually because it's not backed up by a *real value*. Now, that's just absurd. As in the example, we clearly saw that the value of the hypothetical property was not determined by adding up the total cost that was incurred to build the property. It was determined by the *demand* for it in the market.

Now as cryptocurrency continues to gain a widespread acceptance, its demand is soaring and it will only continue to go higher and higher in the coming years. Thus, based on its increasing demand, you can very well imagine the ascending value of cryptocurrency!

"[Bitcoin] is a remarkable cryptographic achievement... The ability to create something which is not duplicable in the digital world has enormous value...Lot's of people will build businesses on top of that."

Eric Schmidt – Executive Chairman of Google

1.5 – How Does Cryptocurrency Lure Investors
Why should people invest in cryptocurrency?

That's another common question that people often ask when you're trying to convince them about the revolution that cryptocurrency has already brought in the financial world. The easiest answer to that question is that an investment in cryptocurrency represents a huge opportunity.

Any cutting-edge business idea progresses over the years gradually from one stage to another until it reaches its maturity. Considering that, cryptocurrency has only reached its infant stage yet. There's a very long way to go before cryptocurrency reaches its maturity and earns global acceptance. But the path for cryptocurrency's global acceptance has already been paved.

If you're in doubt, you can always see the increasing usage of cryptocurrency. More and more businesses are starting to accept payments in Bitcoin. Every day there are announcements by online stores that they also have adopted this new mode of payment. Since cryptocurrency is far from reaching its maturity stage, it's a wise decision to invest in it now and wait for your return on investment (ROI) to be doubled within a few years down the road.

Chapter 2 – Trading Cryptocurrency

Cryptocurrency trading is a rewarding activity, but like stock trading, it sure does involve various risks as well. If you're just starting out fresh in cryptocurrency trading, then trying to grasp some of its basics would help you a lot. Like investing your money in stocks and commodities, you have to play this game very carefully as well. After all, you'll be investing your hard earned money into the market.

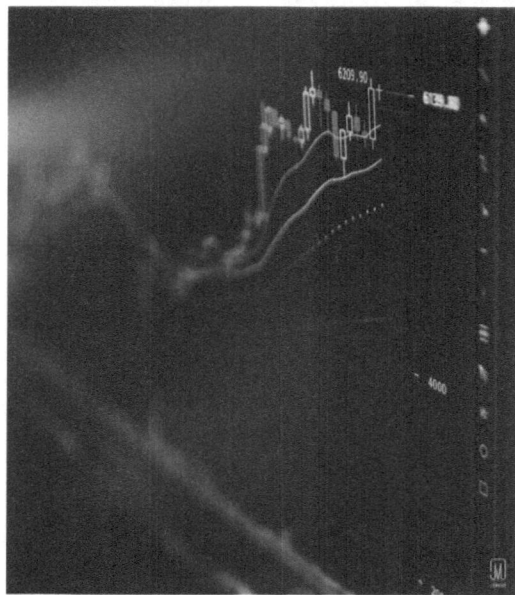

Nowadays, cryptocurrency trading is hailed as the next big thing. It's more popular than ever. A plethora of investors have already jumped into the market and every day few others jump in as well, expecting to earn some easy money.

The first warning for the potential investors would be that cryptocurrency trading is not a shortcut for getting rich and accumulating wealth by any means.

Sure, it does offer you handsome return on investment, but sometimes the risks involved make you taste the bitter taste of a financial loss as well!

There are plenty of reasons why digital currencies are gradually gaining momentum and popularity in the world. However, one of the biggest reasons is the finite supply of these currencies that has been brought to interested investors' attention. For instance, there will ever be only 21 million Bitcoins. Once all of them have been mined, the supply of Bitcoins will essentially stop. Unless some changes are made in Bitcoin's protocol and a larger supply is allowed.

FYI – 80% of all Bitcoins have already been mined and only 20% of the total supply remains to be mined!

2.1 – The First Lesson to Learn Before Trading

The best way to go about crypto trading is to do your thorough research before you dive into these risky waters. Research all you can about the type of cryptocurrency you want to invest in. Never take the risk of putting your money into something you feel dubious about. First, gain confidence and then start the game.

The first lesson for a beginner in crypto trading must be about understanding the prevailing rules of the game. See, there are several benefits of trading crypto, and these benefits are considerably different from trading traditional currencies. In crypto trading, the governments do not have any ability to intervene and banks do not have any authority to freeze your trading accounts. Moreover, the anonymity of crypto transactions makes it very difficult to track the accounts of the users. Aside from these benefits, you must always be aware of the volatile nature of this currency.

When you've done your homework and you think you're ready to test the waters, then it's time for you to choose the two most essential things – a cryptocurrency wallet and an exchange to trade the currency on. You can even create two e-wallets and select two cryptocurrency exchanges if you want. In case you forgot what I mentioned in the previous chapter, your wallet will store all the encrypted passwords and will represent your coins. It's pretty much like keeping your money in a bank account.

2.2 – How to Choose a Cryptocurrency Exchange

The best way to understand the role of a cryptocurrency exchange in this whole game is to compare it with a stock exchange. Crypto exchanges are websites which are basically a platform to buy and sell coins, or exchange them for another digital currency. These exchanges are also where you can convert your cryptocurrency to fiat currencies, like U.S. dollars.

Is it necessary to open an account in a cryptocurrency exchange?

Yes, it is! If you want to do professional trading, then you'll have to. However, if you're not quite serious about crypto trading and if it's just an occasional thing for you, then you can opt for other platforms which do not require an account in crypto exchanges.

Now to choose a cryptocurrency exchange is a tough nut to crack! There is a huge variety of crypto exchanges to select from. The one thing you need to be aware of is that not all exchanges are created equally. This means they do not operate in a similar way. The best way to select an exchange is to gauge the individual performance of each exchange and the services that they offer. The one you think suits your interest the best is the one you should go with.

Now allow me to introduce you to some of the most popular crypto exchanges operating today:

- **Coinbase:** The Coinbase platform is the most secure exchange of them all. It's backed by the most trusted investors and is used by millions of users worldwide. Coinbase makes buying, storing, and trading your coins very secure.
- **Kraken:** If you're exchanging Bitcoin in Euro volume then Kraken is the platform for you. Founded in 2011, Kraken is the largest Bitcoin exchange which also happens to be a partner in the first cryptocurrency bank. You can buy and sell Bitcoins on this platform and you can trade your Bitcoins for U.S. Dollars, Euros, British Pounds, Canadian Dollars, and Japanese Yen.
- **Poloniex:** Launched in 2014, Poloniex is another one of the largest cryptocurrency exchanges that are leading the way. Poloniex has its unique strengths. It offers a secure environment for trading more than hundred different Bitcoins and its pairings with other cryptocurrencies. Its unique tools and data analyses make it a preferred choice for many *advanced crypto traders*.
- **Bittrex:** A platform that supports both established and emerging (or relatively new) currencies. This unique option by Bittrex provides the user a myriad of investing and trading opportunities.
- **Gemini:** With names like Cameron and Tyler Winklevoss behind it, Gemini is a fully regulated and licensed U.S. Bitcoin and Ether exchange. Its regulatory standards are very similar to banks.

Even though the role of a cryptocurrency exchange is similar to that of a regular stock exchange, it doesn't mean they both operate in similar ways. The mechanics of the entities are completely different.

The trading of fiat currencies is bound by its set hours. However, there are no such limitations in crypto trading. You can access crypto exchanges any time you want and trade the digital currency you want to trade at any hour of the day. Also, the trading volume is never constant in the crypto market. It differs during the day because the traders enter the market from different countries at different times. Such fluctuations are not of much significance and have a minimal impact on trading.

So what else should a novice crypto trader know about crypto trading?

There are other essential details that you should be enlightened with. You see, there are events in crypto trading that can most assuredly make your heartbeats race. If truth be told, your heart might skip a beat in such events as well. This happens when the *crypto market skyrockets or declines by huge percentages* in just a matter of a few minutes or hours! This is when you realize that cryptocurrency trading isn't at all free from risks. Trading digital currencies can actually put your capital at stake.

That said, it shouldn't discourage or scare anyone away from the crypto market. Not even the beginners! Like I mentioned before, every investment has risks and every trading market has spikes that can create outcomes you never expected. Same is the case with crypto trading, except that in the crypto market, the degree of volatility is *higher!*

Chapter 3 – The Cryptocurrency Market

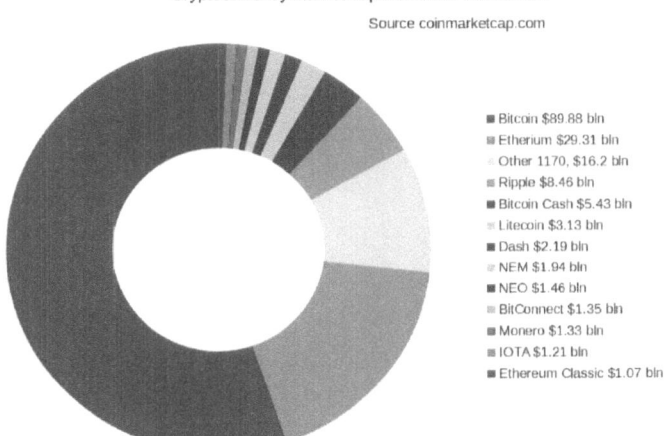

The first decentralized digital currency that left the entire world in a state of shock and awe was Bitcoin. Ever since its inception in 2009, the currency has come a long way and it still continues to grow in value. It's true that Bitcoin did suffer several setbacks that weighed its value down before it managed to reach the price it is at today. Once the faltering baby steps of Bitcoin became firmer and steadier with time, a plethora of other digital currencies marched out and joined the cryptocurrency market, following the lead of Bitcoin.

As of today, it's safe to say that the revolutionary coin market is the fastest growing asset class. You can compare it to real estate markets, stock markets, and bond markets and you'll see that all of them are constrained by geographic and national borders. As for the cryptocurrency market, it doesn't know the first thing about boundaries. Cryptocurrency, by all means, is a global market.

3.1 – The Growing Crypto Market Is a New Frontier of the Financial World

Bitcoin, the mother of all coins, had a 1500% growth in 2017. This massive growth has piqued the interest of traders, investors, and entrepreneurs, making them curious about the cryptocurrency market more than ever. However, it's not very difficult for a newcomer to get lost in this overwhelming market.

With a total capitalization of billions of dollars, the cryptocurrency market rewards all those investors generously who have the courage to delve into it. Since its inception, cryptocurrency has always been speculated to be a financial bubble in the making that will sooner or later burst, resulting in unimaginable losses. The critics of digital currency have predicted countless times that this loss would be the greatest financial loss the world would have ever seen. However, considering the capitalization variables of the crypto market, it gets very clear that digital currency is here to stay and will continue to grow in the years to come.

One pivotal factor to take notice of is that the crypto market is a deregulated market. Many investors consider this to be a favorable thing because it makes investing in cryptocurrency quite simple with very few requirements to take care of. There are some crypto exchanges that even allow you to invest without going through their KYC (Know Your Customer) protocol.

But there's a downside to this as well!

Being a deregulated currency, cryptocurrency is not backed by the SEC (Security and Exchange Commission) or any other regulatory body. This makes the safety of cryptocurrency investments a responsibility of the investor. You cannot hold any authority responsible if your coins are stolen from your wallet due to a security breach or a hack.

3.2 – The Mighty Bitcoin

Bitcoin is the leading cryptocurrency – everyone knows that. *It's the top of the class.* Owing to its reputation, Bitcoin has a significant influence on the overall crypto market behavior. This simply means that if Bitcoin goes up, you can very expect the other currencies to follow the upward trend. This also means that if there's a decline in Bitcoin prices, then it will become very difficult for the other coins to appreciate in value.

3.3 – Understanding the Volatility of the Cryptocurrency Market

If you have experience in stock trading, then it's probably not going to be of much use in the world of cryptocurrency. The only reason for that is the large volatility swings in crypto trading. It's also imperative for a crypto trader to understand that this volatility is subjective. In the stock markets, a drop of 10% in a day is considered unstable and very volatile. However, in cryptocurrency markets, a drop of 10% in a day is considered to be normal.

So does this high volatility make the cryptocurrency market risky?

The volatility in the crypto market is both good and bad. Though it's often cited with a negative connotation, the reality is that without volatility, you can't make money. The volatility is what that makes crypto prices move. In all honesty, it's all about analyzing the market trends carefully and being prepared. It's not a miracle that some smaller capped coins double in price in just a few days. It happens all the time. But on the other hand, if you're not prepared you can also lose your money!

To this day, many people consider cryptocurrency markets a wild trading platform. It's a new frontier and thus, it's labeled *dangerous*. But since the coins are riskier when compared to the stock market, the same coins also pay you higher returns as well. *High risk equals high reward!*

3.4 – The Fear of Investing and the Risk Involved in the Crypto Market

"Virtual currencies, perhaps most notably Bitcoin, have captured the imagination of some, struck fear among others, and confused the heck out of the rest of us."
Thomas Carper – U.S. Senator

The imagination and fear mentioned in the quote by Thomas Carper is basically the result of frequent and unpredictable price fluctuations of cryptocurrency. But as a matter of fact, these fluctuations are not at all random. The prices of cryptocurrencies can be determined by several specific factors. If you study these factors cautiously before investing, chances are you might not suffer a significant loss.

So what are those factors that affect the prices of cryptocurrencies?

When it comes to investing in cryptocurrency, you can always count on government announcements, media propagations, press statements, news events, advancements in technology, increasing or decreasing demand, and the entire crypto community that comprises the developers and users of cryptocurrency. These sources are reliable indicators that can predict whether the crypto prices are expected to appreciate or depreciate in the next few days.

The instilled fear in the minds of people regarding cryptocurrency investments, is it justified?

People have been making stories about the impending crash of cryptocurrency, particularly Bitcoin, since the currency was in its development stage. But if we study Bitcoin prices, all those speculations and predictions are proven wrong. Bitcoin has always managed to bounce back from all downward correction of its prices.

Since July 2017, Bitcoin has enjoyed a 500% increase in its price. The investors who must've closely followed and paid attention to the sources mentioned above would have made a fortune by now!

3.5 – What Is a Cryptocurrency Market Correction?

Although cryptocurrency has penetrated the mainstream, many people still have no idea what a cryptocurrency market correction means.

Market correction refers to the decline in the market capitalization or the value of an entity. Even though there are renowned companies, like Microsoft, Red Cross, and Dell, that have started to accept Bitcoin now, there are factors that are still able to cause its market correction. This correction always results in the reduction of Bitcoin prices.

South Korea implementing harsher cryptocurrency trading rules, China banning crypto trading altogether, and India's finance minister declaring sanctions against cryptocurrency transactions are all first-rate instances of a cryptocurrency market correction. All these incidents caused a sharp decline in the value of cryptocurrencies, especially Bitcoin.

3.6 – How Is a Cryptocurrency Market Correction Healthy

There is another way of looking at the market corrections. The way that makes these corrections look like a healthy sign. But first, you need to understand that inexplicable spikes in the values of all cryptocurrencies have terrible implications. Such spikes in the value can make a cryptocurrency look like a scam. For instance, when Bitcoin's total worth was valued to be $1 billion, it was considered nothing but a financial bubble. Thus, to make Bitcoin a practical source of carrying out transactions, a cryptocurrency market correction was more than necessary.

So does this mean a cryptocurrency market correction is important?

Yes, indeed!

- When Bitcoin was a new opportunity in financial markets, there were only a handful of people had the guts to become a trailblazer by adopting it almost immediately. As Bitcoin gained more popularity, its prices went high and this made it more difficult for the new investors to buy it. Thus, market corrections created opportunities for such new investors to invest in Bitcoin.
- A cryptocurrency market correction does more than just creating investment opportunities for newly interested investors. It also gives them a chance to diversify their

investment portfolio. In January 2018, if you remember, Bitcoin reached an all-time high with its price soaring at the $20,000 mark. However, the market corrected that down to $10,000 approximately. After having seen the recent jaw-dropping increase in Bitcoin prices, this was the chance for the fresh investors to make their move.

- There's another fact that proves a market correction every now and then is indeed healthy for cryptocurrency. And that fact is streamlining – making cryptocurrency free from any turbulence or extreme fluctuations in prices. This extreme volatility is the number one reason for fear of investing in cryptocurrency, and a market correction can mitigate that fear.

The conclusion of it all is that as the demand for cryptocurrencies continues to increase in the global markets, their prices will be corrected by various external factors. Thus, the ultimate benefit of a cryptocurrency market correction is that it maintains the currency at a reasonable price, preventing it from reaching an overly inflated price.

Chapter 4 – Initial Coin Offering (ICOs)

As cryptocurrencies are becoming stronger and growing in value each day, you will be hearing the term "ICO" more often now.

Your next question should be – what's an ICO?

4.1 – Getting Acquainted with the Concept of an ICO

ICO is Initial Coin Offering!

If you have been trading in the stock market or if you've been following the financial section of any media, you must have come across the term IPO – Initial Public Offering. If you haven't, it doesn't matter. IPO is the first time a company sells its stock on the public market. Initial Coin Offering is almost the same thing. It's the first time a cryptocurrency is sold to the interested public. And that's where the similarities of between IPO and ICO end. There's a big difference between the two offerings as well. *IPOs are heavily regulated and ICOs are not all regulated.*

So what purpose does an ICO serve?

Considering the lack of regulation in the crypto world, an Initial Coin Offering is the best way to raise money for a cryptocurrency venture. You can bypass all the rigorous and strenuous capital raising processes involved in the traditional startups and opt for an ICO instead.

4.2 – How Does an ICO Work

Once a cryptocurrency firm decides to launch a new currency, it has to raise capital through an Initial Coin Offering. The process of ICO initiates by making a white paper which includes the following details:

- What is this project of a particular firm all about
- What project would be achieved upon the completion of this Initial Coin Offering
- What is the cost of this project
- What amount of virtual money the startup personnel and the originator will keep
- The acceptable type of money for the purpose of this Initial Coin Offering
- What will be the duration of this Initial Coin Offering

Now as the ICO campaign commences, the supporters, enthusiasts, and the believers of the cryptocurrency will line up to purchase the firm's tokens with either virtual or other types of currency.

FYI – these tokens are to ICO what stocks are to an IPO!

If the firm is able to meet the minimum funding requirements within the stipulated time frame, then the firm will continue working on the project. Generally, if the funding requirements fail, the money is returned to the investors and the ICO campaign is deemed unsuccessful.

4.3 – Why Does ICOs Deserve Your Attention?

There's no need to sugarcoat the risk that exists in the ICOs. Being clear and straightforward, *ICOs are risky!* But if an ICO goes the way it should, its rewards can very easily outweigh its risks. This is why ICOs are gaining traction these days.

I know ICO can be a little difficult to understand. Take a look at this example in order to have a better grip on the concept under discussion.

Say suppose you have $10. In order to keep this simple, let's imagine you bought 10 coins from 10 different cryptocurrency firms when they were conducting their ICO campaigns. To be specific, each coin that you bought from each firm was of $1.

Now 9 out of 10 firms were not able to meet the minimum funding requirements within the scheduled time frame. This means you incurred a loss of $9. However, the tenth firm's ICO was a success and the value of its each coin is now $100.

To sum it up, you lost $9 because you invested at their ICOs which didn't turn out to be successful. However, you managed to gain $100 on the coin you bought at that one successful ICO. This makes your total earning or profit to be $91 ($100 - $9).

Were you able to understand that despite the inherent risk involved in ICOs, why you must still pay attention to such campaigns? The above example was a hypothetical one. It was given to make you understand a bigger and a real-life scenario.

In 2014, the Ethereum project was publically announced. During Etheruem's ICO, the firm raised Bitcoins.

Those Bitcoins were worth $18 million. Back in those days, each Ethereum had an approximate value of $0.40. When the Ethereum project met the minimum requirements as per the schedule, it went public by 2015. Then in 2016, Ethereum gained immense popularity which increased the value of each Ether coin to $14.

Now that was actually a jaw-dropping increase in value!

Let's say you had invested $100 at Ethereum's ICO, this means your investment would have reached a high of $3,500 in just less than two years.

Now you must have noticed that even though there's a high risk in Initial Coin Offerings, the reward is just astonishingly high. This is exactly why investors are so drawn into ICOs.

Now it's worth bringing into your knowledge that since Initial Coin Offerings are deregulated campaigns, it's possible that you might become a victim of a scam. In such a situation you'll lose your money and there will be no legal action for you to take.

But this shouldn't dishearten you at all.

The deregulation of ICOs makes it very convenient for everyone to buy virtual coins without any specific requirement or qualification! However, it is highly recommended that you should only invest in trustworthy ICOs and invest only the amount of money you can afford to lose.

4.4 – Attracting Potential Investors for an ICO

Considering that ICOs are about selling digital currency, the ideal way to attract the potential investors is to select a platform that will prove to be the best for your ICO. This is the first step and the most vital one of all. Selecting the right platform (like CoinLaunch for instance) out of the hundreds that are available today will determine the fate of your ICO. If you're selling digital currency on a right platform, the chances are you might be able to sell it at a remarkable gain. Considering that ICOs are not regulated, it's possible for you to launch your ICO in any country. However, in order to make sure that investors are attracted to your ICO, you must be certain that you're providing an environment that is conducive to efficient trading.

4.5 – Why You Might Regret Not Investing in an ICO?

There's an invisible marketplace that seems to be growing at an unprecedented rate. The exponential growth of this market is doubling the initial investment in just a few days or weeks at most.

You guessed it right. It's Initial Coin Offerings that I'm talking about!

Most of the people still think they've seen and heard it all before – it's a "so-called" gold rush where the only person getting rich is the one who sells the shovels. See, your skepticism is 100% legit and it's fine to be a cynic because digital currency isn't a widely understood phenomenon as yet. But what if this is not a hoax? What if this time you really have a shot at hitting the jackpot? Will you be able to forgive yourself that you missed a real chance of multiplying your invested money? After all, investing in ICOs is rewarding the investors in ways beyond imagination!

4.6 – The Advantages of an ICO

It's true that virtual currency is taxable. All the capital gains that you earn from exchanging your digital currency for dollars are taxed. But there's more to investing in ICOs than fearing the tax that will be imposed on your capital gains.

- An ICO is in many ways comparable to an IPO, but it's relatively easy to invest in an ICO. To buy shares of a company you would have to open an account with a stockbroker and this means you would have to deposit thousands of dollars to open that account. Only then you'd be able to buy stocks at retail prices. In ICO, there's no concept of a stockbroker or a broker account. All you have to do is buy tokens with your Bitcoin, Ethereum, or any other cryptocurrency at affordable transaction costs.
- ICOs are not bound by geographic borders. It means that an Australian can purchase the tokens of an American based cryptocurrency firm without having to jump through lots of hoops. However, the same person cannot easily purchase the shares of an American company at its IPO while living in Australia.

- For those who still run after earning profits by investing in IPOs, the potential for earning profits is way much higher with ICOs than those traditional IPOs. You must be thinking how. Well, ICO's are a lot easier and less expensive for companies to launch and for investors to participate. That's why more investors and sellers come together in ICOs, driving the prices higher.

When the automobile was invented, it slowly changed the whole concept of traveling for the human beings. Then the world went through another revolution when computers came along and the internet followed. We all know what happened next, our lives were changed forever. Similarly, we're on the cusp of yet another revolution that will be brought into our lives by cryptocurrencies and ICOs very soon. These are just the initial stages of that revolution. You just wait and see!

Chapter 5 – Introducing Altcoin

"Virtual Currencies may hold long-term promise, particularly if the innovations promote a faster, more secure and more efficient payment system."

Ben Bernanke – American Economist

Altcoin is a term that stands for *"alternative coin"*. Altcoin, you can say, is a standard name or an umbrella term used for all advanced digital currencies other than Bitcoin.

5.1 – Why Do Altcoin Exist?

To sum the purpose of altcoin in a few words, altcoins were introduced as and still remain a competitive preference to Bitcoin.

One pioneer altcoin called Namecoin was launched in the cryptocurrency market in 2011, soon after the creation of Bitcoin.

Today, Namecoin is just one of more than 1,300 altcoins circulating in the market!

The ultimate goal behind Namecoin's creation was to decentralize the domain registrations. Namecoin still ranks high among other prolific altcoins and is also used as interest for a digital money installment.

As of now, there are many altcoins in the market that are fundamentally same as Bitcoin. There are quite a few functional properties of altcoins that are similar to Bitcoin:

- They are created through the same mining procedure.
- They are decentralized currencies because they depend on a shared system.
- They have proven to be more effective and less expensive methods for trading.

Altcoins came into existence for some other specific reasons as well for which they are used even today.

For instance, altcoins are frequently used to subsidize new companies instead of giving specific offers that can support the startup businesses financially. There's an altcoin called AI-COIN which offers a steady flow of profits and first-rate investment opportunities by using a unique two-stage strategy. The first stage is to trade cryptocurrencies using artificial intelligence for earning short-term gains. The second stage is to invest those earnings in the new AI enterprises and the emerging companies in public blockchain space.

5.2 – Which Altcoin Is the Best Altcoin?

With more than 1,300 altcoins listed on the cryptocurrency exchanges, it's exceptionally difficult to determine which one of them is the best altcoin out there in the market. However, this doesn't mean that all the altcoins trading in the cryptocurrency market are similar in terms of their value. Only a small number

of altcoins are worth your consideration. If you want to try and identify which altcoin is truly a blue blood investment then there are a few important factors that must be taken into account.

In order to judge the worth of an altcoin, it's really important to determine if any organization offers that altcoin to its clients or not. Whether or not that organization cares about the masses will also help you form a better opinion about the altcoin it uses. Then the next factor that ascertains the worth of an altcoin is the group of developers behind the currency. It is highly essential that the altcoin developers are reputable, creative, and committed to the cause.

The most crucial factor that decides the value of an altcoin is whether its transactions are easily settled or not. A good altcoin should not trouble you when you want to convert it into fiat currencies. You need to make sure that a particular altcoin is safe from any sort of extortion, and that it's protected against online thefts.

5.3 – Why Do People Keep Creating Altcoins?

The first reason why cryptocurrency developers keep on creating altcoins is that Bitcoin certainly has its share of issues. This makes people believe that the digital currency system can be improved further. For instance, trading Bitcoin can result in high fees. Moreover, Bitcoin transactions can take a considerable amount of time to be processed on the exchanges.

Thus, these flaws in Bitcoin led to the creation of altcoins, out of which some of them are designed to reduce the transactional expenses and increase the speed of processing fund transfers.

There happens to be another solid reason behind the creation of an uncountable variety of altcoins. This reason might sound a bit cynical, but it's actually not. It's just more money related. As Bitcoin continues to increase in value, crypto investors look at the cryptocurrency market with sparkling dollar signs dancing in front of their eyes.

Thus, this insatiable hunger for money compels people to launch their own digital currency and step into this money making business.

Once their altcoin can easily be mined, they can sell it if there's a drop in its value and earn a tremendous amount of profit!

5.4 – Some of the Most Popular Altcoins

With so much fluctuating *FUD* around Bitcoin, it is always hard to predict the market for Bitcoin.

By the way, if you're interested in cryptocurrency, then you better get accustomed with the acronyms commonly used in the world of cryptocurrency. Let FUD (Fear, Uncertainty, and Doubt) be the first acronym you learn.

Ever since cryptocurrency was unveiled in 2008, there has been a proliferation of digital currency companies and codebases. Using the advanced blockchain technology, hundreds of promising altcoins have emerged up till now. However, only a few of them have proven themselves to be true contenders to the mighty Bitcoin.

Given that there's an intense competition between altcoins, it's always interesting to see which altcoin falls into a shadow and which one stands the test of time.

Before I move on to introduce you to some of the reigning altcoins of today, let me make this clear that making a list of bankable altcoins is a very challenging task. There are so many of them. Thus, this list of altcoins is not exhaustive by any means and is subject to change with time because most of the emerging altcoins continue to play musical chairs with each other.

5.4.1 – Ethereum

Ethereum is considered as the fiercest rival to Bitcoin. Created by the alliance of giants like J.P. Morgan Chase, Microsoft, and Intel, Ethereum cannot be classified as just a currency. It's basically a blockchain platform that is powered by the Ether cryptocurrency. The main purpose behind the creation of Ethereum was to program binding agreements into the blockchain. The concept has now incarnated into the very popular smart contract feature.

5.4.2 – Ripple

This Google-backed altcoin garnered a large amount of venture capital when it was still at its inception stage. The ICO of Ripple was able to pull more than $50 million from banking institutions alone. Ripple impressed the market with its total collected funds that rounded up to about $90 million. Ripple is a unique digital currency, it allows its users to transact with any unit of value – it can be a fiat currency or even frequent flier miles.

Ripple offers global financial settlement solutions by enabling the world to exchange value like it exchanges information over the internet. Thus, the currency has given a rise to the internet of value (IoV), i.e. blockchain. Ripple solutions have lowered the total cost of

financial settlements by allowing banks to make direct and instant global transactions with the certainty of settlements.

Ripple was a middle tier currency, but it has now gained epic momentum in the crypto market. In fact, last year in late March, Ripple experienced a 100% increase in value within just a 24 hour period!

5.4.3 – Litecoin

Charles Lee, a former Google engineer, created Litecoin with the intention of coming up with an improved version of Bitcoin. It's true that with Litecoin, the speed to generate a new block has dramatically improved because it uses an alternate confirmation calculation that happens to be more reliant on memory, while Bitcoin has always depended on processing power. Owing to that, Litecoin transactions are four times faster than Bitcoin.

Even though Litecoin was designed to speed up transaction authentications, its fast speed makes its blockchain larger and more susceptible to producing orphaned blocks. Simply put, orphaned blocks are detached blocks that are not a part of the main chain as they are created when two miners generate blocks at the same time, or when someone with enough hash power attempts to reverse transactions.

5.4.4 – DASH

DASH is a combination of two words – *"digital"* and *"cash"*. The currency is known as the internet's cash-in-hand because DASH is really fast and its transactions are instant. According to the claim made by the developers of DASH, time is valuable, thus, InstantSend payments of DASH are confirmed in less than a second.

Ironically, it can take up to one hour for Bitcoin transactions to be processed!

Mining DASH is not cost effective if you use the GPU and CPU mining. You will need special computers known as ASICs to solve DASH's proof-of-work puzzles.

5.4.5 – NEM
NEM is slightly different from the rest of altcoins. It is written in Java and is built on a completely new codebase that is entirely separate from Bitcoin's open-source code. Some other intriguing differences come to your attention when you compare NEM with Bitcoin. For starters, you don't mine NEM, you harvest the currency. It's basically the same as mining in Bitcoin, but in harvesting, multiple people can make profits in small quantities when a new block is generated.

5.4.6 – Ethereum Classic

Ethereum Classic is a parallel platform for Ethereum users. It came into existence when the Ethereum community got polarized over a disagreement pertaining to the handling of a technically legal theft of funds. The majority of Ethereum users were of the opinion to change the currency's code to get their lost funds back. However, a minority of users believed that Ethereum should not be tampered with or altered by involving third parties. They wanted the blockchain to remain *immutable* even if the users continue to exploit Ethereum's smart contract feature. Thus, the users in minority created this version of Ethereum.

5.4.7 – Monero
Monero is an altcoin that was created to target the cryptocurrency users who demand greater anonymity in their transactions. With Monero, you can send and receive funds without making your transactions visible on the blockchain. Owing to Monero's leveraging of ring signatures, your transactions remain completely untraceable.

But this anonymity in transactions comes with darker realities. It is because of Monero's emphasis on extreme privacy that the currency has been adopted by the darknet and various other criminal organizations.

5.4.8 – Zcash
Zcash operates on the same privacy standards as Monero. However, unlike Monero, Zcash transactions are shielded and are not made completely private. This means, the details of the transaction, such as the user's ID and the traded amount, are hidden not kept confidential. The optional secrecy of user's profile is maintained in Zcash by using zero-knowledge proof which allows the users to exchange funds without having to reveal each other's identity.

5.4.9 – Decred
Decred is an altcoin that focuses on open governance, community input, and sustainable funding and development. The currency has melded proof-of-stake and proof-of-work mining algorithms to ensure that a minority of Decred users do not end up owning the majority of the funds and that the crucial decisions regarding the currency are taken by the community rather than the developers of Decred or its early investors.

5.4.10 – PIVX

PIVX means Private Instant Verified Transactions. This is yet another open-source and decentralized blockchain based currency. It was built and still thrives upon Bitcoin Core.

The developers of PIVX state that people have the right to make global transactions that are secure and private, without any interference from the corporate world, government, and the nefarious individuals with prying eyes. PIVX, like Monero and Zcash, also boasts its heightened security and privacy, but it's also known for its high volatility. Moreover, because of its high privacy levels, PIVX is a vulnerable altcoin prone to criminal activities.

Out of the many that exist, these altcoins are the ones that heavily dominate the crypto market.

People in the mood of investing in altcoins must assess their risk tolerance. Sure, altcoins are a valuable short-term trading asset, but they're only for those investors who have patience and knowledge. You need to be absolutely certain that the altcoin you're investing in is the most viable coin for you. Thus, due diligence on your part is a must before you invest in an altcoin.

Altcoins can also prove to be a rewarding long-term asset. However, you must perform a thorough analysis of the digital currency environment before you decide to hold altcoins for a period longer than a year.

Chapter 6 – Mining Coins

People might have started to hear about cryptocurrency, like Bitcoin and Ethereum, but they're still unaware of how the blockchain protocol is responsible for generating new coins.

Mining the cryptocurrency coins and maintaining the crypto transaction platform are the jobs assigned to the miners, also known as the node operators.

6.1 – Cryptocurrency Transactions

I mentioned how digital currencies run on blockchain technology in the first chapter. A blockchain is operated by independent mining operators from all over the world. When you want to make a transaction using the Bitcoins in your wallet, you'll first have to send a query to the miners who will authenticate the transfer of your funds.

Miners process a crypto transaction by checking the balance of an e-wallet, as recorded in the master ledger (blockchain). If the coins are enough to process the transaction, the system will resolve the query. The cryptocurrency protocols are designed in such a way that each query takes a specific amount of time to be successfully resolved. For instance, the time that a Bitcoin query takes to be resolved is set at ten minutes.

The authentication of a cryptocurrency transaction involves solving a cryptographic problem. Once this complex mathematical code is solved, it allows a pending block of transactions to be added to the blockchain, where the entire history of crypto transactions is recorded.

All crypto transactions are taken as an input that is run through a hashing algorithm. For instance, the hashing algorithm that Bitcoin uses is SHA-256. This hash function produces an output called a hash. In simple words, a hash is a code akin to a mathematical problem that the miner has to solve. The rate at which a mining computer works out these problems is referred to as *hash rate*.

In the case of Bitcoin, hash rate, which is also referred to as hash power, is the unit that denotes the speed that the miners on Bitcoin network are consuming to solve the Bitcoin code within the set mean time of ten minutes.

The required calculation to solve a particular cryptographic code is performed simultaneously at hundreds of connected nodes. The first mining computer to solve that code adds the solution to the blockchain. The updated ledger is then sent to other miners on the network for authentication. The authentication means that a crypto transaction has been verified by the majority of nodes and is updated on the blockchain. The mining system that successfully works out the correct solution to a hash code earns a fraction of the coins involved in an authenticated transaction.

The mathematics involved in hash algorithms used by cryptocurrencies ensures the anonymity of crypto transactions. Once a transaction is run through a hash algorithm, it's not possible to generate original data from its generated hash, because a hash function only functions in a linear progression. An easy analogy to understand this would be that you cannot possibly create a real human thumb from a thumbprint. That's why a hash is considered to be a *digital fingerprint* of the transaction that is processed through a hashing algorithm.

6.2 – The Art of Mining Coins

Mining basically involves two operations. The first one is authenticating crypto transactions for existing coins, which we just discussed, and the second operation is generating new coins. Like in authenticating transactions, solving a complex cryptographic problem is also involved in mining new coins.

One might ask – what purpose do these mathematical problems serve exactly?

The primary objective of these mathematical puzzles is to find the most efficient way of adding a new block to the ledger. Moreover, this method has been adopted to generate new coins because it provides the least incremental value to the currency.

When mining new coins, it's better to have a higher hash rate because it increases your chances to find the next block and earning the set reward. The reward for the first mining computer that solves a cryptographic code is a small amount of newly generated coins. These awarded coins are then added to the total circulation of the coins.

6.3 – Difficulty in Mining Coins

As it turns out, it's not that easy to mine coins. This is perhaps the most challenging phase of using cryptocurrency. Every cryptocurrency developer continues to add a certain degree of difficulty and cost to its mining operation, as with time the number of miners joining a cryptocurrency network keeps on increasing. The cryptographic puzzles are getting more and more difficult in nature and harder to solve as the hash rate of advanced mining computers is increasing. This model is designed keeping in mind the real world business situations.

You might be wondering how the mining model of cryptocurrency is similar to the real business world.

There are more barriers to entry and lower profit margins for each business in an industry that is highly competitive. On the other hand, an industry that comprises few sellers tends to give a considerably high return on investment.

This is exactly how the functioning of the cryptocurrency world may be defined.

The next pertinent question in your mind should be – can mining be done on ordinary computers?

No!

Mining new coins is not a regular activity. It requires advanced computational resources, such as computers with high-tech processors and graphics cards.

Thus, before stepping into the world of cryptocurrency, you must be financially sound in order to bear the cost of buying and operating such expensive resources.

Here's a brief scenario that illustrates the most recurring difficulty faced by the new Bitcoin enthusiasts:

Bitcoin is a digital currency whose value is of constantly fluctuating nature. When the value of Bitcoin rises, mining suddenly becomes a highly pursued activity in order to generate an income that can be earned because of the fractional reward system.

This is when the crypto enthusiasts realize that mining Bitcoins is actually more profitable than their day job! So they gather all the money they can and buy the necessary equipment to become miners, at least for the time period during which Bitcoin prices are high.

But like I mentioned above, when the number of miners increases, the level of difficulty of mining Bitcoins also goes high. The crypto puzzles get tougher. Such complex mathematical problems require more advanced machines to solve a hash code. Moreover, the profits are marginalized when the costs due to scalability issues for each competing miner continue to increase.

As a result of this predicament, miners will have to stop mining Bitcoin once the constantly rising costs become too expensive for them to bear.

Although not all cryptocurrencies use blockchain technology, this self-correcting system lies at the heart of all digital currencies. However, this system is what that keeps the crypto market from getting oversaturated with coin mining operations.

Chapter 7 – All You Need to Know About Staking Coins

"Cryptocurrencies take the concept of money, and they take it native into computers, where everything is settled with computers and doesn't require external institutions or trusted third parties to validate things."
Naval Ravikant – Founder and CEO, AngelList

The inception of blockchain-based cryptocurrencies has provided an alternative and lucrative way for people to make money. The fact of the matter is that digital currencies have eliminated the need for relying on stock exchanges and depending on traditional brokers. There are millions of people around the world who are making money by means of crypto trading, mining operations or *staking coins*.

7.1 – What Is Meant by Proof of Staking Coins?

Proof of Staking (PoS) is somewhat the latest consensus algorithm for some cryptocurrencies. It creates new blocks that are added on the blockchain. A person who already holds some coins is able to stake these new blocks and can validate a new transaction on the platform.

The other way to understand the concept of Proof of Staking is that a person is in the position of mining or validating block transactions depending on how many coins he or she owns. For instance, the more Bitcoin or altcoin are held by a miner, the more validating power that miner has.

7.2 – How Does the Process of Staking Coins Work?

In an ordinary crypto network, like Bitcoin network that is based on Proof of Work (PoW) mining, transactions are processed randomly by the mining node that solves a complex algorithm at the end of a timeframe in the minimum amount of time. Thus, it's not up to investors who own Bitcoin to decide or select which network operator gets to validate a Bitcoin transaction. Only the mining node that is first to work out a cryptographic code can validate a transaction.

However, in Proof of Staking protocol, miners are randomly chosen from a pool by owners of the digital coin. In case you're wondering how a miner can be added to the pool, it can easily be done if you are able to stake a certain number of coins in a bound wallet.

When a mining node stakes the coins in a bound wallet, it creates a new block that is always proportional to the percentage of coins staked. For instance, if the number of coins staked by a mining node is 5% of the total coins that exist on the network, then that node can only validate 5% of the total transactions in a new block.

7.3 – The Benefits of Staking Coins

The process of staking coins has proved to be beneficial for mining operators in many ways:

- The consensus mechanism has removed the need for buying high-end computer hardware. When a mining node stakes bound coins from a crypto e-wallet, it is guaranteed a fixed number of transactions on the network for validation, regardless of its processing power.
- Those investors who have enough investments in the coin are authorized to validate transactions on the network.
- Unlike ASIC and other mining hardware, the value of coins staked through Proof of Staking does not depreciate with time. If there's anything that can affect the value of staked coins it is fluctuations in prices of digital currencies.
- As it turns out, Proof of Stake is more energy efficient and environmentally friendly than Proof of Work mining on which Bitcoin network is based.
- Proof of Staking is also super safe. Staking coins system has reduced the threats of 51% digital thefts and attacks.

The most fundamental benefit offered by Proof of Staking to mining operators is the riddance of the need to buy any expensive hardware. This new system is a predictable source of income for miners. It offers them a guaranteed return unlike

Proof of Work system where the coins are awarded randomly to the most advanced computing systems.

7.4 – The Risks Involved in Staking Coins

There is only one drawback associated with staking coins in a bound wallet. The staked coins are locked up for some period of time and cannot be sold. This may not seem like a problem when the value of the coins is increasing, but it may result in a loss if the price is falling. Owing to this risk, the amount earned through staking would not be enough to cover the depreciation of price during a bearish run.

7.5 – Popular Cryptocurrencies for Staking Coins

With coin staking, digital currency holders get some power on the network. That power is related to the ability to earn a regular income on their investments. If you have trouble understanding how that's done, then consider it very similar to receiving interest for keeping money in a bank account.

The ability to stake coins in order to get mining preference is favored by crypto investors. In fact, many new digital currencies have built this model into their platform.

There are many digital currencies that are considered good for staking coins, but here a few most popular ones.

7.5.1 – DASH

We all know DASH is a popular digital currency and it stands for "digital" and "cash". DASH was one of the first digital currencies to introduce coin staking mechanism. Initially, DASH was built on the core of Bitcoin. Once the currency got popular, further improvements were made by implementing unique features, like PrivateSend and InstantSend.

The investors can stake DASH coins through a masternode and earn an annual return of 7.5%. To run a masternode, the minimum requirement is of 1,000 DASH units. For instance, if DASH is priced at $320, this makes the cost of running a masternode close to $320,000.

If truth be told, DASH is not actually a PoS digital currency, but the masternodes of DASH kind of work in a PoS way which makes its coins very profitable.

7.5.2 – NEO

The idea behind NEO is to create a smart economy by using blockchain technology. The Proof of Stake algorithm used by NEO is dBFT algorithm. Investors on the platform can stake their coins by binding them in a NEON wallet. The investors can expect to earn new NEO coins at the rate of 5.5% annually for all the staked coins.

As of now, NEO is quite a popular digital currency and the number one currency at *Bitfinex*, a Chinese digital currency exchange based in Hong Kong. Moreover, NEO is expected to rival Ethereum that has occupied the number two position in cryptocurrency markets for a very long time now.

7.5.3 – OkCash

After having been introduced in 2014, OkCash, that has been designed to be suitable for carrying out micro-transactions, has an excellent return on investment on staking. OkCash coins can earn a return of 10% annually on the value of the stake. This return is considered to be the highest return among other PoS digital currencies. As of now, OkCash is trading at $0.121 in the markets.

7.5.4 – PIVX

PIVX (Private Instant Verified Transactions) was forked out of DASH in 2016. Now, it is established as a fully PoS digital currency that allows staking on the blockchain and gives its investors a decent annual return of about 5%. The most important thing to know about PIVX is that you can stake any amount because there is no cap on it. This is actually a very good low-entry barrier.

7.5.5 – NAV Coin

NAV Coin is one of a kind cryptocurrency because it has a dual blockchain for carrying out private transactions. Moreover, NAV Coin is a functional PoS cryptocurrency that came out in 2014 as Bitcoin's core code. Some of the unique attributes of NAV Coin include fast transactions that can be carried out in not more than 30 seconds, optional privacy due to its dual blockchains, and an excellent PoS rewards system that gives you an annual return of up to 5%.

7.5.6 – Stratis

Stratis is another PoS cryptocurrency that simplifies the creation, testing, and deployment of C# applications on the dot NET framework. STRAT is the token that runs Stratis platform. STRAT can be staked by using a Stratis wallet to earn annual returns of up to 0.5-1%.

It's true that the annual returns for staking Stratis are quite low when compared to its competitor currencies, but if you have a considerable amount of STRAT, then you can earn a handsome profit by staking it. There is no cap for staking STRAT.

7.5.7 – Reddcoin

Reddcoin has become the tipping digital currency of social networks. Using Reddcoin, a PoS cryptocurrency, you can easily tip anyone for developing any type of content that you prefer on numerous social media platforms. Of course, being a PoS digital currency, Reddcoin can also be staked in a wallet that gives its holders a decent annual return of about 5%. Reddcoin also does not have a cap for staking.

Staking PoS digital currencies is the latest and smartest way to earn passive income. The best thing about doing so is that in the case of many cryptocurrencies, the entry barrier is quite low to get started.

Think about it. Earning 1% to 5% free reward is absolutely not bad at all, considering you don't have to do anything except for keeping your wallet open.

When there exist zero and negative interest rates in some countries, like the United States, then cryptocurrency staking naturally turns out to be more profitable.

Chapter 8 – The Crypto Wallets

"At their core, cryptocurrencies are built around the principle of a universal, inviolable ledger, one that is made fully public and is constantly being verified by these high-powered computers, each essentially acting independently of the others."
Paul Vigna – Reporter for the Wall Street Journal

A crypto wallet is an e-wallet where you store your coins. This simply means that each cryptocurrency user has a software address where the coins are kept in a safe custody. A secret key is given to the crypto users to access their coins and make a transaction.

It's entirely up to the users how they prefer to safeguard the secret key to their crypto wallet. You can either store it electronically or write it down on a piece of paper provided that you are able to remember where you put it.

A crypto wallet can be online and offline! Fascinating isn't it?

Online wallets can be further classified into two types – a wallet that is easily accessible at various locations, and a wallet that can be stored on your personal computer. On the other hand, an offline crypto wallet can be an equipment based wallet. It's almost the same as a memory card or a removable drive that can be accessed by using a USB port. Essentially, these wallets enable people to own cryptocurrency.

Cryptocurrency wallets are very much similar to the tangible wallets that all of us carry in our pockets to carry cash and credit cards. The only difference is that crypto wallets cannot be seen, and they carry money that also cannot be seen!

Considering the fact that cryptocurrency depends on codes, the safest method to keep your wallet protected and secure from being taken over by unauthorized users is using the good old paper-based option.

Just like banks have account numbers and names for their different types of accounts, digital currencies have unique addresses to each wallet on the blockchain. Each wallet has a public address and a private address. The public address is used to acquire tokens and coins and the private address is used to access your wallet to send tokens, coins, and make transactions.

If it wasn't for cryptographic wallets, digital currency would not have become such a widely acclaimed phenomenon. The means of keeping the currency safe is what that has made people embrace the idea of advanced currency in the first place.

8.1 – Types of Cryptocurrency Wallets

Even if the inability to remember the complex keys to crypto wallets has made many people dubious about using cryptocurrency, it hasn't stopped them from buying and storing the coins. It's difficult to trust your memory with such complicated secret keys. It's true your memory can fail you when it comes to remembering such details. Most of the people who bought Bitcoin when it was new didn't use it in those days. It was only when Bitcoin prices went high that these people realized they had forgotten the key to their wallet. People who had written their key on paper had already lost that piece of paper by the time Bitcoin prices eventually skyrocketed. People ended up losing millions this way.

However, this was when people had no idea how big a digital currency Bitcoin will become with time. Now that cryptocurrencies have become the talk of every town, people and their memories are less likely to forget the keys to their crypto wallets.

There are three types of crypto wallets to store cryptocurrency. These wallets ensure that there are minimum security threats to your coins.

8.1.1 – Hardware Wallets

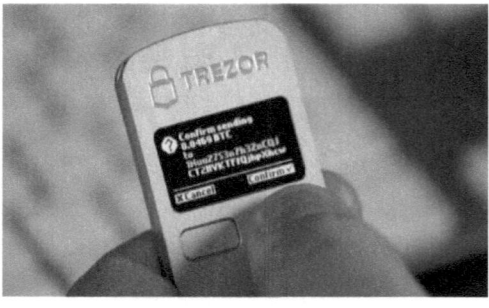

Hardware wallets hold your private keys offline in *cold storage*. This means there is no connection to the internet. Thus, your wallet and your currency are kept safe from the reach of all the malignant programmers and hackers. A hardware wallet is set up with a *seed expression*.

A seed expression is a series of words unique to each cryptocurrency user. It helps regain access to wallets if by any chance you lose or damage it.

The setup of a hardware wallet is quite simple. All you have to do is connect your wallet to a USB port and download the required software.

Hardware wallets are considered the most secure means to keep your coins safe!

Most of the hardware wallets have default software, but there are some that require separate software to connect to your computer. A hardware wallet can be expensive. Thus, it is a considerable option only if you own and want to store coins worth a significant amount of money.

8.1.2 – Software Wallets

Software wallets are based on computer software. These wallets are available in three formats:

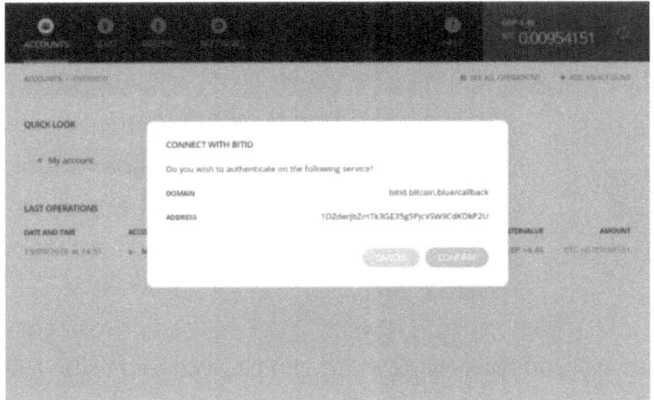

- **Online** – These are web-based wallets that run on the cloud and provide the easiest access to your currency from anywhere and any device. These wallets store your private keys on the web and are controlled by a third party. This is why online wallets are vulnerable to the threats of professional hackers and online thefts.
- **Mobile** – These wallets are operated by apps on your smart-phone. With mobile wallets, you can access your digital currency easily if you want to use it at a retail store.
- **Desktop** – These wallets are downloaded and kept on your personal computer. They require no third party interface, which means you have a complete control over your digital currency. Even though desktop wallets provide high levels of security, if your PC is hacked or is infected with a virus, there is a solid chance that you might lose all your coins.

Some software wallets are designed to store one type of digital currency, while others can store multiple kinds.

8.1.3 – Paper Wallets

The simplest form of Bitcoin wallet is a paper wallet. It's just a piece of printed paper that contains a cryptocurrency address and your private key that can be accessed using a QR code. These are cold wallets. This means they have no security threat of being hacked because they are not connected to the internet. Also, a paper wallet is the least expensive way to store digital currency.

Paper wallets have one major drawback!

If you lose your paper wallet and you haven't created a backup, there's no way to restore access to your coins.

8.2 – Maintaining Crypto Wallets

Now that there are uncountable cryptocurrencies you can trade with, is it necessary to maintain a separate wallet for each cryptocurrency?

Yes! It is absolutely necessary.

Each type of digital currency that you own demands its own digital wallet where coins can be securely stored. If you have invested in several cryptocurrencies, then it gets difficult to keep track of each wallet.

Why is it difficult? You would ask.

Each currency has its own wallet and each wallet has its own key which needs to be kept safe and protected. But as cryptocurrencies have gained popularity in the mainstream, the whole process of storing the coins in wallets and using wallets have been made simpler. Extensive efforts and time have been invested to make the system more refined, effective, and efficient by improving the security levels and by reducing the time it used to take to access crypto wallets.

8.3 – How to Choose the Best Crypto Wallet

The different types of cryptocurrency wallets exist for a reason. Not every type of crypto wallet is suitable and appropriate for everyone. You must take into consideration the following features when you have to choose a digital wallet for your use.

- **Compatibility** – It's highly necessary the wallet you choose is compatible with different types of operating systems.
- **Security Features** – One cannot imagine having a crypto wallet with poor security features. It would have disastrous consequences. Thus, the wallet you choose must have the best security protocols. Also, make sure you seed the backup keys and PIN codes on priority.
- **Regulate Private Keys** – A crypto wallet that you choose for your personal use must allow you to store your private keys safely and securely.

There is no such crypto wallet that can store all types of digital currencies that you own. Thus, you have to determine which type of wallet will be suitable for you based on which coins you own.

There's no need to mention this, but it's extremely important that you, as a crypto wallet owner, never share your private key or wallet password with anyone. There's only one person who needs to know these details about your crypto wallet, and that's you only!

Chapter 9 – Cryptocurrency & Marketing

"If you care about liberty, the nonaggression principle, or economic freedom in general, you should do everything you can to use Bitcoin as often as possible in your daily life."
Roger Keith Ver aka "Bitcoin Jesus" – An early Bitcoin investor

Cryptocurrency opened the doors for entrepreneurs and various business owners. It is true digital currency has created new opportunities and ways of doing business. Traditionally, you had to go under a considerable financial debt or sell the shares of your company to raise funds. Today, thanks to ICOs, entrepreneurs can raise funds worth millions of dollars more effectively and efficiently.

The best feature of ICOs is that they enable businesspersons to raise funds without carrying the burden of debt and without having to deal with the bureaucratic SEC.

Indeed, cryptocurrency and ICO have brought a legitimate revolution in economics. And both these things are here to stay!

However, just by conducting an ICO, there is no guarantee of success. With each passing day, ICOs and cryptocurrency markets are getting competitive and increasingly difficult to manage as more and more entrepreneurs are converging towards this new vehicle to raise capital.

Most of the entrepreneurs fall in love with the *big idea* of conducting an ICO and raising money for their new business. They think if they have a lucrative business idea, they can conduct an ICO and funds will come flowing in. However, the reality is not so simple. The problem is that many entrepreneurs ignore the most important aspect of the whole plan – *effective marketing*.

So effective marketing is the solution to this problem?

Of course! If no one knows you're conducting an ICO campaign, who is going to buy the tokens? In a nutshell, there will be no demand for your currency. Make no mistake about it – creating demand makes you the king in any market, especially in the cryptocurrency market. It's the demand that will increase the value of your Initial Coin Offering.

Now we're coming to the crux of this book – effective marketing is the fundamental element that increases the value of your ICO and your digital currency!

9.1 – How Does Marketing Increase the Cryptocurrency Value

So far, it has been established that marketing is very crucial for the success of your ICO and digital currency. It can prove to be fatal if you overlook how marketing can significantly increase a cryptocurrency's value. Now it's time to examine the reasons as to why this is the case.

9.1.1 – Increases Visibility

This is probably the biggest reason why entrepreneurs need to invest in marketing. In fact, not just invest, *heavily invest!* Your ICO campaign needs to get attention and visibility as much as possible. But that doesn't mean all forms of marketing will have a similar effect on your ICO.

The truth is that some methods of marketing have become a cliché and are considered outdated. Such methods can end up hurting the launch of your digital currency. Thus, instead of running the risk, consider investing in a modern marketing firm that is aware of the contemporary norms of marketing. Such marketing firms understand and implement only those marketing strategies that would work best in a specific scenario. A successful marketing strategy results in a dramatic spike in the interest levels of crypto investors, driving the demand for your digital currency up.

9.1.2 – Establishes Authority

Marketing is a tool widely used to create demand and sell almost anything. In the case of cryptocurrency, effective marketing can establish and increase the authority of the digital currency you're launching. These days, almost anyone can design a striking website and make fantastic claims. And people have developed a sense for this. Thus, they look for authority and credibility before they spend their money. In the case of an ICO, crypto investors are interested in entrepreneurs that precisely understand the business venture they are embarking upon and know how to articulate it.

Marketing helps you create that reputation in the market.

With dynamic marketing strategies, you can convincingly communicate your status as a preeminent expert in a specific field. Such entrepreneurs are considered professionals and are perceived as authoritative figures. As a result, the investors you're trying to hook will amass trust and confidence in you and your business. The end result of this will also be an increase in demand for your digital currency.

9.1.3 – Builds Rapport & Trustworthiness

You must not forget that no matter how popular cryptocurrencies get, they're still considered infamous because they are exempt from being controlled by regulating bodies. This induces a fear in people's minds that digital currencies are susceptible to digital thefts and that there's nobody who can stop scammers and hackers from entering the market. This is a huge factor that holds people back from investing in cryptocurrencies, especially in the ones that are new and don't have a significant presence in the market.

Marketing helps people build faith and confidence in new cryptocurrencies. It gives such currencies a platform to gain prominence, build rapport, and establish a reputation as a promising digital currency in the eyes of crypto investors in order to attract them, win their attention, and tempt them into making an investment.

It's common sense. Why would scammers put themselves through the fatigue of running lengthy marketing campaigns? This is why when you make marketing efforts, potential investors see you with less suspicion. You're not a questionable entity to them because you're marketing your business endeavors.

Marketing spreads the word, making others recognize your integrity. This spikes the demand level of your upcoming ICO because *value* is basically *perception*. People who will participate in your ICO and invest in your business by buying your digital currency will do so considering the future value of your company.

Marketing helps you create the perception that the future value of your business will soar!

9.2 – Digital Marketing for ICOs

By now, we understand that Initial Coin Offering (ICO) is the new and exciting way of raising funds that can turn your business idea into a reality. And an integral component of a successful ICO is *digital marketing*.

The last thing a growing business needs is a debt or the complexities of the SEC. An ICO is free from all these things. It's free from the regulations of the SEC. But this also goes against ICOs because it makes digital currencies riskier. Thus, in the case of digital currency, it's the responsibility of an investor to ensure if an ICO is a sound investment or not. This is why, when you're conducting an ICO, it's mandatory that you present your company as an honest and reputable one. This will make your ICO attractive enough to tempt investors into buying your coin and will increase the influx of capital as well.

Digital marketing is the best tool that you can use to run promotional campaigns and present your company as a reliable one. This is how you should lay the foundation of your digital marketing campaigns:

- **Promote a Major Investor** – Potential investors will feel secure if a major and influential investor is investing in your company. Make sure you promote that investor as a part of your team.
- **Get in Touch with the Community** – You're launching a new currency. It's going to make some ripples in the market. So be active on all social media platforms to keep your followers posted on the latest developments and to answer their queries and concerns.
- **Build a Solid Team** – Smart investors have an acute sense of identifying a great and trustworthy team. They know it's what that leads a business to the path of success. Thus, assemble a team comprising the best and most qualified members to represent your company.

Once that's done, it's time to put your digital marketing efforts into top gear.

9.2.1 – Optimize Your Website for Search Engines

This is very critical, especially when you're operating in an unregulated industry. There are instances where a fraudulent website ranks above a legitimate one. You need to make sure this doesn't happen with your website because investors will sense a scam and will back off. Nobody wants to lose their money after all. And you can't blame the investors who visit the fake site and believe it to be the real deal. The word will spread around soon, tarnishing the reputation of your company.

9.2.2 – Put a Lot of Effort into Your White Paper

White paper serves as a proposal to potential investors. And smart investors know how to evaluate a white paper. They can tell by reading a white paper if a company is worth their investment or not. If you prepare a mediocre white paper, this will lead investors to believe that you are a mediocre entrepreneur and that your coins are not to be trusted with their money. Thus, it's imperative to spend some quality time writing your white paper.

9.2.3 – Make a Credible Explainer Video

Attracting the attention of potential investors is a big challenge. This is why you must provide features to investors that can build their trust with your company. Make a video that explains the objective of your ICO and what your company is trying to achieve. An explainer video will capture the most attention and will make you sound credible.

9.2.4 – Start E-Mail Marketing

This is something you should be doing from day one! E-mail marketing is a great way of sending updates to your investors. Some of them might eventually become ambassadors for your ICO as well. There's a reason why e-mail marketing has stood the test of time. Because it works!

9.2.5 – Use Social Media to Your Advantage

Social media is an extremely powerful tool in today's world. Everyone is present on at least one social media network. This is the platform where you can build an intimate relationship with your investors and potential investors as well. It's the latest and most dependable method of relaying information.

It's true that ICOs hold the potential to revolutionize how companies raise capital. But this does not mean that the moment you launch an ICO, investors will rush to buy your tokens. You need to disseminate the information about your ICO to as many people as possible. With these tips in your mind now, you should have the basic understanding of how to execute a successful digital marketing campaign for your ICO.

9.3 –

Webinar – An Effective ICO Marketing Strategy

ICOs are being adopted in industry after industry to raise funds for diverse business projects. ICOs are also becoming common in the FinTech (Financial Technology) industry. In 2017, capital worth over $5.6 billion was raised through ICOs. This money was used to launch more than 400 successful business projects that reached their intended targets.

If truth be told, the ICO method of raising funds was first brought to attention by Ethereum back in 2014 when the project was successful enough to raise more than $11 million in its presale. Other successful cryptocurrencies that were launched later on, like Ripple, DASH, and Stellar, were able to raise a higher amount of investments during their presale and ICOs.

We can learn how to plan and run a successful ICO marketing strategy by looking at and learning from the examples of ICO platforms that did exceptionally well and made history.

Moreover, we can also learn valuable lessons – what NOT to do when trying to launch an ICO – from the examples of projects that failed.

9.4 – Why Are Webinars an Effective Marketing Strategy for Launching an ICO

An ICO, like an IPO, requires a lot of marketing efforts. Most of the companies that are looking forward to raising funds through ICOs happen to be well established in their respective domains. Their history of operations, profitability, and management experience is enough to market their ICOs. The marketing efforts carried out by such companies only have to communicate these strengths to the public.

However, new companies that are coming up with diverse and innovative business ideas have to put their heart and soul into their marketing efforts in order to convince potential investors. Such companies have to communicate their business idea, its benefits, and their goals to the general public. Everyone understands your company is trying to make huge profits. That's the purpose of running a business in the first place. What exactly is your company trying to achieve in the market and how does it intend to achieve that over a period of time is what needs to be relayed to the public. In fact, other important details, like your company's long-term vision and objectives also need to be communicated.

Once you have completed your planning and have identified the company goals, its technological expertise, and its competitive advantage that needs to be explained to the public, the next step is to select a suitable medium to communicate your message to investors. There are three immensely useful methods that have proven to be very effective in getting your message across.

The first method is to bring social media platforms into your use. This is where you can easily find the majority of people who are interested in ICOs. Thus, you have no better avenue than social media to market and promote your ICO project.

The second method is to develop a website that has blogs about your ICO project and other quality content. This website will serve as your digital address and will help you in the process of creating trust and authenticity for your ICO. Moreover, your website will allow your potential investors to get in touch with you directly and find out more details about your business idea.

And finally, we zero it down to the third method – webinars. A webinar is a highly effective method to introduce your standout ideas and unique vision to investors.

9.5 – The Importance of a Webinar

Webinars and live presentations should become the center of your focus and your marketing efforts, once you have created your website and have taken control of your social media presence.

The good thing about webinars is that they allow you to directly present your ideas and promotional messages to an audience of investors and pique their interest. However, to think your job is done after conducting one webinar is not appropriate. Webinars should be conducted frequently to update people and inform them why they must invest in your business. You can initiate a very strong dialogue on the value your company is intending to offer.

Face to face communication says a lot of things that written communication cannot. Facing your audience and delivering a message builds a lot of trust and reputation. You look confident about your business endeavors. A website and social media presence cannot go that far in building your image. Investors are more likely to trust you and your business idea if they can attach a face to it. Conducting a series of webinars humanizes your ICO and gives your investors an opportunity to ask you questions directly.

One of the things to learn from successful ICOs is that investors feel more confident trusting you with their money when the promoters are able to answer their questions openly during live online communication. Any prudent investor will consider an ICO shady and misleading if there is no face attached to it.

9.6 – Learn from Other Successful ICOs

If you look at some of the successful ICOs, you will notice that there were more than a few experienced promoters and marketers behind them. The point is that you will have a hard time forming a core group of supporters behind your new digital currency if you're the only one talking about it and promoting it everywhere.

It's the diverse talent of multiple promoters that make an ICO a big success. Your technical expert will be better able to handle specific questions pertaining to platform design, while your financial expert would explain the competitive advantage offered by the new platform like a pro.

If you want everyone to be talking about your ICO and if you want your digital currency to become a sensation, then involve the news media. An interview or a target story with a renowned media group will significantly help your ICO.

Yes, the idea sure is expensive, but the boost in popularity and public interest is definitely well worth the price. In fact, if you do things in a smart way, you may not even have to pay anyone to get the media attention. The media will take notice of your ICO on its own! It only takes one reputable crypto media outlet to run a story on your successful ICO, and the rest of the news websites will be running after you to do an interview with them as well.

9.7 – Digital Tokens

Blockchain-based crypto tokens have made life easier for everyone. These tokens can be conveniently traded over an openly accessible P2P network.

There are two things that you need to get a token. First is an internet connection and second is an e-wallet that is assigned to a specific IP address.

People who have crypto tokens can trade them to anyone in the world in just a matter of a few minutes. Holding crypto tokens is very secure. They cannot be stolen as long as you follow guidelines on keeping your tokens safe. Blockchain technology has made it possible to maintain a complete record of transactions that have ever taken place on a network. That is why, considering our current technology level, blockchain platform is famous for maintaining the most accurate record of digital transactions.

9.8 – Using Reddit as an ICO Marketing Tool

"I think there will always be need of trusted voices in the investment community, but what the ICO markets are showing is that the world has incredible demand for future-looking projects!"

Adam Draper – CEO and founder of Boost VC, a crypto and VR (Virtual Reality) startup accelerator

These days, ICOs are all the rage. Even though the SEC doesn't ever stop discrediting the idea of ICO and there are some disclosure requirements now, many companies continue to launch their own ICOs.

The main idea behind conducting your own ICO is to launch your own specific brand of crypto tokens that can be easily used and traded over your company's blockchain platform.

According to the reports from the crypto world, more than $4 billion has been raised in only the first quarter of 2018 through ICOs. Looking at this number, there's a very good reason to believe that this is just the beginning of a global trend as more and more businesses continue to launch their own digital tokens.

9.9 – How to Promote an ICO on Reddit

Just as Bitcoin is the most reputable and popular cryptocurrency, *Reddit* is undoubtedly the most admired message board on the planet! Stylishly called the "front page of the internet", the Reddit website is visited by millions of users across the world in a single day.

Something this famous and widely accessed by people around the world has to be one of the most brilliant platforms to promote an ICO. Thus, it becomes extremely important to understand how you can run a promotional campaign on Reddit for your ICO.

With a very active community of users, Reddit is the ideal message board that can be used to propagate and publicize new ideas and businesses. Reddit site is subdivided into more than a hundred thousand message boards called *subreddits*. When it comes to cryptocurrency, one of the famous subreddit on the website is "Altcoin Discussions".

As you must have guessed, Altcoin Discussions is a message board dedicated to cryptocurrencies other than Bitcoin. This subreddit is also an excellent place to announce the upcoming crypto coins through the announcement thread. The announcement thread allows companies to introduce their ICO tokens to the entire world.

What must a good announcement thread have in it?

A good announcement thread includes an easy to understand summary of the token, its purpose, and the details pertaining to the support network that is backing the coin.

There are specific details that the summary must include, like the maximum coin limit and a trustworthy introduction to the development team behind the coin. If one of the developers has any previous experience with cryptocurrencies, it's good if that experience is advertised and brought to investors' attention. This will prove to be an important factor. A new token that has an experienced team of developers behind it will generate greater investor interest. Thus, such information becomes absolutely relevant to promote an ICO on Reddit.

9.10 – Creating a Subreddit for Your Coin

In order to spread the word and develop the interest of investors so that you may have a successful coin sale, it is extremely important that you promote your token well in advance of your ICO. Not just when the date of your ICO has come close. For this, you must create a subreddit for your coin.

The company launching its own coin uses Reddit message boards as a company prospectus that allows developers and supporters of the coin to communicate and discuss all relevant news and updates regarding the token to future investors and other interested parties.

If a company is successful at creating and running an active message board on Reddit that gets updated regularly and provides all information regarding the coin development, there is no better tool out there than Reddit that can build investor confidence and support for the coin soon to be launched.

Another benefit of using Reddit for the promotion of your coin is that the users may also spread the word around to other altcoin communities. This is possible because Reddit happens to use a voting-based algorithm for the purpose of advertising a discussion that's being run on the platform. This way the topics with many up-votes tend to get displayed higher in search results for users.

9.11 – Engaging with Your Reddit Audience

You must be thinking there must be some way to keep your subreddit followers entertained and hooked to your cause.

Well, that's right. There are a few ways to keep your audience interested.

The best way to attract lots of potential investors to your token is to invite diverse questions from your target audience. The progress of your token and development reports will be enough to keep your supporters on board.

And there's something even better than that!

If you want to turn fringe supporters of your coin into true and core believers, then you would have to actually engage them with your development team.

Now how can you do that?

9.11.1 – Encourage Your Subreddit Followers and Attend Them

What you must do is encourage your subreddit followers to find out more about your project. You can do this by letting them ask you a variety of questions about your business idea and ICO.

Once that's done, the ball is in your court. And it's time for you to impress your audience.

You can do that by making sure that you're active on the message board. You must answer all the queries in an absolutely timely manner. This will leave a solid impression on your supporters and will show them the extent of your seriousness in your project.

9.11.2 – Dealing with Supporters' Feedback

There's one thing that you cannot certainly ignore – the feedback and suggestions given to you by your subreddit followers. You have got to take your supporters' feedback and suggestions about your project and ICO into consideration. The fact is that the crypto community on Reddit is really wise and quite knowledgeable. Thus, many members of Reddit crypto community can help you by offering a great advice that you can follow in order to improve your Initial Coin Offering.

9.11.3 – Dealing with the Criticism

All the criticisms that you get on your subreddit about your project or ICO must be dealt with professionally and with a positive attitude. The thing is that if people are going to invest their hard earned money into your token, your company needs to show them what makes your project a standout idea that is unique and certainly better than others. The most important thing while dealing with Reddit audience is not to get angry and lose your temper when someone negates your token or your business idea.

9.12 – Buying Up-Votes and Advertising on Reddit

It's true that Reddit, like any other social media platform, is a business. The company allows Reddit users to purchase up-votes for your subreddit. You can very well imagine what happens when your subreddit gets many up-votes. Your subreddit is considered well-marketed and is displayed higher on search results.

Reddit also allows positive responses to be displayed higher than those negative comments that you may have received for your business idea or ICO. That's just good and favorable advertising. Some companies have also confessed about buying moderators who can swing the position of negative and positive posts on their subreddits.

Is it fair to buy up-votes and change the order of positive and negative posts on your subreddit?

Well, it's not highly recommended to take this route for marketing, but if you're really keen on promoting your ICO on Reddit, then options such as these are certainly available.

Conclusion

"I think the internet is going to be one of the major forces for reducing the role of government. The one thing that's missing, but that will soon be developed, is a reliable e-cash."

Professor Milton Friedman – American economist

Blockchain technology is here to stay and revolutionize the world. However, many people across the globe are unaware of its existence and what exactly it is capable of doing.

"Blockchain is a technology that allows anyone to send anyone else a piece of information, currency or data in a secure, transparent and anonymous way."

Douglas A. Boneparth – President and founder of Bone Fide Wealth

Although cryptocurrencies have dominated the news and headlines of the recent past, it's actually blockchain technology that is used to trade these digital coins and that's what will continue to develop in the years to come. Cryptocurrencies happen to be just one product of blockchain technology.

The fact that blockchain transactions do not involve a middleman or financial institution resonates with the masses deeply. Furthermore, these transactions are irreversible, intangible, secure, instant, global, and they do not require any permission from some authority.

And do you know what the best thing about cryptocurrencies is? There is no representation of financial debts in digital currencies.

Once people get to fully understand blockchain technology, all their mistrust and doubt that still exists when it comes to virtual currency transactions will gradually diminish. And they will gladly embrace the modern future.

That day is not very far when blockchain technology will be used to carry out medical and real estate transactions. It wouldn't be surprising if voting would also be conducted via blockchain technology. It's going to change our lives radically like the internet did.

So are you ready to take a step into a more advanced future?

Krohn Media
http://krohn.media

www.ingramcontent.com/pod-product-compliance
Lightning Source LLC
Chambersburg PA
CBHW030449220526
45464CB00006B/2459